TARTANS
The Facts & Myths

by Libby and Blair Urquhart

JARROLD PUBLISHING

INTRODUCTION

Tartan once identified those who wore it as Highlanders, a warrior race from the northern part of Scotland, deemed savage yet noble. An image invested with the virtues of honesty and loyalty that has kindled the imagination of both storytellers and historians throughout the ages. Tartan has arrived in the twenty-first century strongly associated with the facts and myths of an entire culture, which it has come to symbolise.

Tartan has become the country's national costume, occupying a unique place in its history, and in the hearts and minds of millions of Scots. From the times of the early clansmen through to the traditions of the modern Highland regiments, the kilt, plaid and tartan have constituted the unmistakable costume of the Highlander. The dress today remains most attractive, distinctive, colourful and martial.

However, many aspects of tartan and Highland dress are controversial and the subject is surrounded by a number of myths. For example, the word 'tartan', now associated by most people with the precisely patterned, intricately cross-barred and multi-coloured cloth, is itself a matter for argument. Some authorities claim it derives from the Irish-Scots words *tuar* and *tan*, meaning 'colour' and 'district' respectively. There is also a possibility that the word derives from a Middle French word *tiretaine*, which referred to a quality of material, of a thin, coarse linen and wool mixture. An Old Spanish word of similar root, *tartana*, which means 'shiver' and refers to a very fine, quality cloth, has been proposed as another possible source. The Gaelic word for tartan is *breacan*, meaning 'striped', 'variegated' or 'speckled'. (Robert Louis Stevenson's hero in *Kidnapped* was called Allan Breck; 'breck' meaning 'pockmarked'.)

In Scotland, by the fifteenth and sixteenth centuries the word tartan was being widely used by English and Scots speakers for distinctively woven cloth coming out of the Highlands. In 1538, for example, King

Above: A member of the MacDuff clan, an ancient clan who were the celtic earls of Fife, from a print by R.R.McIan

A piper at Glencoe

James V, the father of Mary Queen of Scots, purchased 'three ells of Heland Tartan'. However, the name seems to have applied to a type and quality of cloth rather than to a design, a usage that had changed gradually by the eighteenth century. Nowadays, tartan is generally defined as a fabric woven in bands of coloured yarn that repeat in sequence, not only across the width but along the length of the cloth. A new hue is formed wherever bands of a different colour cross. It is sometimes said that modern Highland dress bears little relationship to that worn in the past, but this is not the case. All national costumes evolve and what we see today in Scotland is a stylised version of an ancient garb.

A kiltmaker at work

An historical pageant is played out in Highland dress at Glenfinnan in Inverness-shire. It was here that Bonnie Prince Charlie raised the standard at the beginning of the final Jacobite campaign in 1745

EARLY REFERENCES

This engraving – from Louis Simond's *Journal of a Tour and Residence in Great Britain, 1815* – shows Scottish Highlanders in the early nineteenth century

Colours and Dyes

The coarse wool from these animals, which were primarily kept for their milk, was plucked rather than shorn. It was then spun and, using the different natural wool colours, an intricately woven and striped cloth was produced. Originally, the Highlanders used only the natural shades of the sheeps' wool – black, brown or white – in the designs of their tartan cloth. Later they employed a range of leaves, berries, bark and lichens as natural dyes to develop cloth patterns involving many colours. The birch tree, for instance, produced yellow; while the alder produced black or brown; heather gave orange; the crowberry or blaeberry, purple; the bramble, blue; and the flower of the tormentil, red. Urine – *fual* or *graith* in Gaelic – was used as a source of ammonia to deepen and intensify colours and to remove grease. Before the dyeing was completed the wool was always washed and a mordant (from the Latin verb *mordere*, 'to bite') was added to make the dye permanent. The substance used was often the salt of alum, copper or chrome, and iron mordanting was obtained from black peat bogs.

Some of the earliest references to the dress of the Scottish people, the Celts and Picts, appear in the writings of the poet Virgil, and later Roman authors. During attempts by the Romans to occupy Scotland, the Caledonian tribesmen who opposed them wore striped woollen cloaks, or blankets woven in several colours. These garments were draped over a shoulder and pinned, while underneath was a linen tunic shirt and sometimes a pair of truis or breaches. (Usually, however, the legs were bare, giving rise to the later nickname for Scots mercenaries – 'redshanks'.) A piece of cloth found near the Antonine Wall, the third-century Roman barrier that ran from the Clyde to the Forth, is an example of this simple two-coloured check or tartan. It was made from the dark and light wool of the original goat-like sheep of Scotland.

Ancient Campbell (left), and Macdonald tartans

Weaving

There were several main stages in weaving tartan: gathering the wool, preparing the fibres by combing it to the desired texture for soft or hard tartan, and spinning by a method involving a drop spindle, or distaff and spindle, in which the yarn or thread was spun by the fingers and wound round the bottom of the spindle. This was later replaced by the spinning wheel, and ultimately by modern machinery. The wool was then dyed, woven and finally stretched. This last stage, known as waulking, was often accompanied by singing, during which jokes would be made about friends, frequently in impromptu verses; a tradition that has continued into modern times in the Harris tweed industry.

Looms were normally upright, operated by one person, with the warp – the threads running the length of the cloth – fixed along a frame with spaces in between, and weighted at the base. The lateral threads, the weft, were then woven in across the warp. Much faster horizontal looms with foot pedals came into use in the eighteenth century, when the manufacture of tartan became a cottage industry. Production later moved to the mills, with the advent of the Industrial Revolution, where water and later steam-power turned the mill wheels, until eventually tartan manufacture evolved into the highly technical procedure of today. Some of the most important of the tartan manufacturers in the eighteenth and nineteenth centuries, like the firms of William Wilson and Son of Bannockburn and J. & D. Paton, at Tillicoultry, below the Ochil hills, supplied the army with tartan and also exported it all over the world.

Wool weaving for tartan manufacture has evolved from the use of traditional looms operated by one person into a highly technical process. Above the cloth is woven on a modern loom, and below the process continues at a factory in the Scottish Borders

THE PLAID

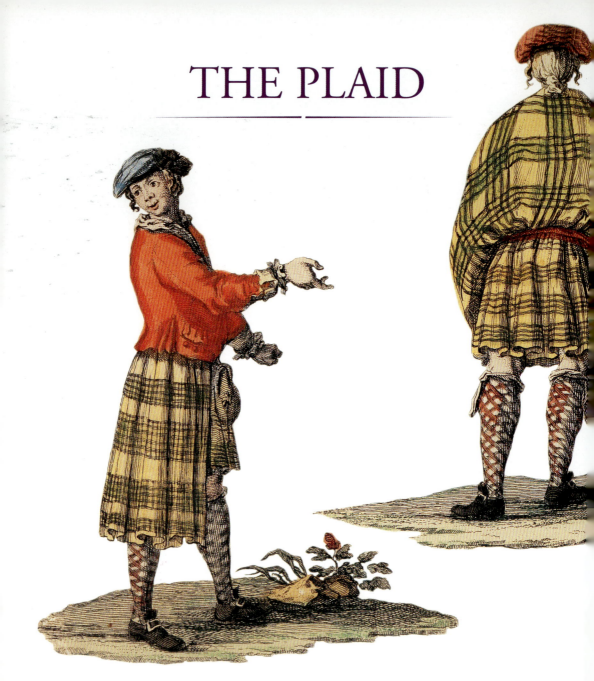

It is not possible to say precisely when the tartan cloak evolved into the long garment known as the belted plaid (and which itself was the forerunner of the modern kilt), but it was probably around the tenth or eleventh centuries. This long plaid was wrapped round the body and was known in Gaelic as the *feileadh mor*, meaning large and folded, or pleated. It was normally made up of two pieces of material, each approximately 4 metres (4–5 yards) long and 70 centimetres (28 inches) wide, the measurements being dictated by the size of the loom. The two pieces of cloth were then stitched together.

It is generally believed that the Highlander put his plaid on by laying it out on the ground with a belt underneath and then pleating it until two aprons at either end remained. He would lay down with the material about knee-height, fold over the aprons and fasten the belt. Then, he would stand up and adjust the rest of the plaid to suit either his mood or the weather.

This French illustration shows the different methods of wearing the plaid

When it was not being used as a cloak, the upper part of the cloth was pinned, but the sword arm would normally be left free. The belted plaid was a superb garment to wear while campaigning. Made of pure wool and closely woven, it was both strong and warm, but could easily be cast aside in battle.

Centuries ago the hem of this garment was higher up the leg than it is today. The plaid worn by the pipers and drummers in modern pipe bands is a stylised version of the old *feileadh mor*.

It is interesting that in North America where the kilted plaid is still sometimes worn as evening dress amongst the members of Caledonian societies, the *feileadh mor* is known as the *breacan feile*, which means 'kilted-tartan' in Gaelic. The word 'plaid' can also carry quite a different meaning in North America, where it is sometimes used to refer to tartan in general. In Britain, however, 'plaid' originating from the Gaelic word *plaide*, meaning a blanket, refers specifically to a particular type of garment.

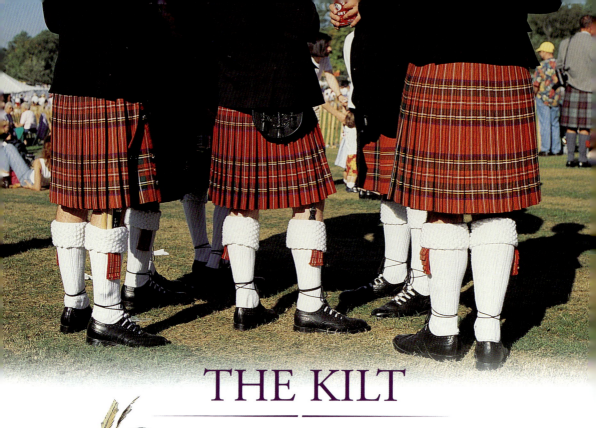

THE KILT

Above and left: The style of wearing the kilt has changed over the centuries

The kilt worn today is the little kilt, the *feileadh bheag* (meaning the 'little fold') from which the anglicised word 'philabeg' derives. This garment originally had large box pleats that were sometimes stitched; while the neat, tight pleats of today's kilt are the result of military influences in the nineteenth century.

The shortening of the *feildeah mor* to a form roughly resembling that of the modern kilt is normally said to have begun around 1725. One story often told is that of a Glengarry furnace-master from England who felt that the long plaid of the Highlander was an industrial hazard and should be cut down. Although this anecdote has been widely told, it seems a far more likely explanation that the little kilt evolved throughout the Highlands simply as a matter of convenience and as the availability of other clothing, such as jackets, jerkins and tunics, increased, rather than as a result of a single incident in Glengarry.

Neil Munro (1863–1930), the author of two magnificent historical novels, *John Splendid* and *The New Road*, portrays some of his characters wearing a form of the little kilt in the seventeenth century. His hero, young Elrigmore, has returned to

> We have a way of belting on the kilt in real Argile I have seen nowhere else. Ordinarily, our lads take the whole web of tartan cloth, of twenty ells or more, and coil it once round their middle, there belting it, and bring the free end up on the shoulder to pin with a brooch – not a bad fashion for display and long marches and for sleeping out on the hill with, but somewhat discommodious for warm weather. It was our plan sometimes to make what we called a philabeg, or little kilt, maybe eight yards long, gathered in at the haunch and hung in many pleats behind, the plain brat* part in front decked with a leather sporran, tagged with thong points tied in knots, and with no plaid on the shoulder. I've never seen a more jaunty and suitable garb for campaigning, better by far for short sharp tulzies* with an enemy than the philamore or the big kilt our people sometimes throw off them in a skirmish and fight (the coarsest of them) in their gartered hose* one scrugged bonnets.

Above: An excerpt from Neil Munro's historical novel *John Splendid*
(*Note: brat means an apron section; a tulzie is a clash or fight; hose means stockings; scrugged means tugged firmly down or into place.)

This illustration from 1803 shows William Macdonald, Officer to the Highland Society of Scotland in full Scottish costume

Argyll in 1644 after fighting as a Scottish mercenary in the army of Gustavus Adolphus of Sweden, and is dressing himself to go into the burgh of Inveraray. It is clear from his description (above right) that the modern kilt is simply an adaptation of the belted plaid, stitched up, with two flat panels at the front.

The word 'kilt' may come from Scandinavia. (Many Scots place names are of Norse origin – a relic of Viking days.) Equally it may stem from the Irish word for a screen, *ceilte*. In Scotland the word, both a noun and a verb, was originally associated with a garment of pleats, skirts or folds; as a verb it meant to lift or shape a garment into skirt form.

Centuries ago the dress of Highland men and women evolved along different lines, and the kilt is traditionally considered to be a man's garment. Women do wear the kilt for Highland dancing, and the only difference lies in the degree of shaping at the hip.

Truis

The Highlanders also wore truis, which were a form of tartan trousers rather like tights or leggings covering both legs and feet. These were particularly

This photograph from the late nineteenth century shows a colonel of the 1st Battalion of the Argyll and Sutherland Highlanders

worn on horseback, and sometimes with the belted plaid. Tartan trousers are still worn in some Scottish regiments, but in the strictest sense, these are not truis.

TARTAN AS A WAY OF LIFE

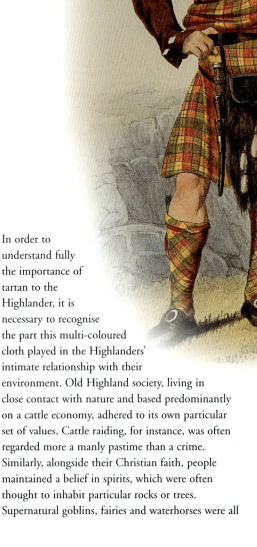

A member of the Buchanan clan, one of R.R. McIan's illustrations for *The Clans of the Scottish Highlands*

In order to understand fully the importance of tartan to the Highlander, it is necessary to recognise the part this multi-coloured cloth played in the Highlanders' intimate relationship with their environment. Old Highland society, living in close contact with nature and based predominantly on a cattle economy, adhered to its own particular set of values. Cattle raiding, for instance, was often regarded more a manly pastime than a crime. Similarly, alongside their Christian faith, people maintained a belief in spirits, which were often thought to inhabit particular rocks or trees. Supernatural goblins, fairies and waterhorses were all assumed to be living beings, and clansmen wore plants or leaves in their bonnets as talismans. (They were not generally clan identification badges, as is often said.) The calendar of the Highlanders, so closely linked to nature, the seasons and to a pastoral lifestyle, was vastly different to that of today.

The material requirements of daily life – house timbers, furniture, beds, tools and eating utensils – were obtained from the natural world. Lamps, called cruisies, were manufactured from fish or seal oil, with rush stems as wicks; the buds of birch could be used as a kind of shampoo. Given the Highlanders' deep affinity with their natural surroundings it is

The photograph above demonstrates how the Highlanders would have slept during a campaign

A member of the MacGillivray clan c.1850, with the accoutrements of battle, in an illustration by R.R. McIan

not surprising that the local wools, colours and patterns of their tartan garments evoked a feeling of intimate kinship with their homeland.

Whenever these cultured, though resilient and warlike people were called to arms, they invariably campaigned in tartan dress. At night they frequently slept in the long plaid and in the 1745 Jacobite Rising they refused to use tents. Sometimes they would soak the plaid in water and wring it out before going to sleep so that a kind of steamy heat was generated inside. In battle, the very sight of the plaid, tartan and kilt caused alarm amongst their enemies, especially during the famed Highland charge, which was a controlled affair of formidable power. (The use of a combination of old and modern weapons – swords, axes, dirks, muskets and pistols – is generally credited to Alasdair MacColla, the renowned military leader of the Clan Donald, and the second in command to the Marquis of Montrose during the Scottish Wars of the Covenant in the seventeenth century.)

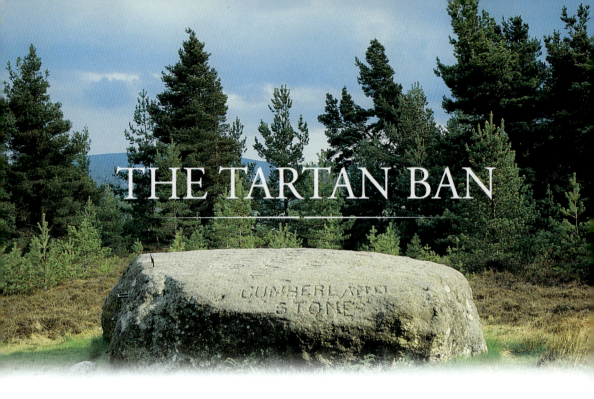

THE TARTAN BAN

The Cumberland Stone stands at Culloden, scene of the final battle of the Jacobite uprisings. The Jacobites were routed by the Hanoverian forces under the command of the Duke of Cumberland, and after the defeat came the fierce reprisals

The Jacobites (from the Latin word for James, *Jacobus*) supported the claim of the exiled House of Stewart to the throne of Britain in the seventeenth and eighteenth centuries. During the risings of 1715, 1719 and particularly of 1745, the Highland clansmen so frightened the Hanoverian government in England that when they were finally defeated at the Battle of Culloden in 1746, fierce reprisals and penalties were exacted on the Highlands. One of the measures, which banned tartan dress, was imposed on all except those in the army or the militia who had remained loyal to the Hanoverian government, and lasted from 1747–82. At the time, the government proclamation read:

THE PROCLAMATION OF THE BAN

In the nineteenth year of the reign of our sovereign Lord George the Second by the Grace of God, of Great Britain, France and Ireland, King, Defender of the Faith…. 1746…. An Act for the more effectual disarming the Highlands in Scotland: and for the more effectually securing the peace of the said Highlands: and for refraining the use of Highland dress.

From and after the first day of August one thousand, seven hundred and forty-seven, no man or boy within that part of Great Britain called Scotland, other than such as shall be employed as officers and soldiers in His Majesty's forces, shall, on any pretence whatsoever wear or put on the clothes commonly called Highland clothes, (that is to say) the plaid, philibeg or little kilt, trowse, shoulder belts or any part whatsoever of what peculiarly belongs to the Highland garb: and that no tartan or partly-coloured plaid or stuff shall be used for great coats, or for upper coats: and that if any such person shall presume, after the said first day of August, to wear or put on the aforesaid garments, or any part of them, every such person so offending, being thereof convicted by the oath of one or more credible witness or witnesses before any court of justiciary, or any one or more justices of the peace for the shire or stewartry, or judge ordinary of the place where such offences shall be committed, shall suffer imprisonment, without bail, during the space of six month, and no longer: and being convicted for a second offence before a court of justiciary, or at the circuits, shall be liable to be transported to any of His Majesty's plantations beyond the seas, there to remain for the space of seven years.

There was immediate and widespread resentment of the measure in the Highlands. Men like Duncan Forbes of Culloden, who had supported the Hanoverian government in the 1745 Rising, and who was Lord Advocate, and Lord President of the Court of Session, tried to stop the ban being implemented. It was widely felt that the humiliation of the Highlanders in this way would be unwise and counter-productive. However, the ban was strictly enforced, causing much hardship. Further legislation was introduced in 1747–8 extending the ban. The plaid, philabeg or little kilt, and tartan itself were all specifically prohibited. The penalties of imprisonment for a first offence and transportation for a second were later changed to enforced military service in Britain's American colonies at a time of growing French influence there. These measures had a seriously demoralising effect on the Highlanders.

THE OATH

I ... do swear, and as I shall have to answer to God at the great day of judgement, I have not nor shall have in my possession, any gun, sword, pistol or arm whatever: and never use any tartan, plaid or any part of the Highland garb, and if I do so, may I be cursed in my undertakings, family and property – may I never see my wife and children, father, mother and relations – may I be killed in battle as a coward and lie without Christian burial in a strange land, far from the graves of my forefathers and kindred – may all this come across me if I break my oath.

Those under suspicion of Jacobite sympathies were asked to take an oath (above), which demonstrated a shrewd understanding of the character of the people.

Repeal of the ban

The ban on the wearing of the tartan was not repealed until 17 June 1782, 35 years later. By this time it was plain that the Jacobite claims to the throne of Britain had ceased to be an important threat. More than two-thirds of the generation that saw the ban imposed had died before it was lifted, which caused much traditional tartan lore to be lost. Fortunately, through the men of the Highland regiments, or militia, tartan survived. These bodies of troops, which wore the belted plaid and the little kilt, and were known as the Highland Independent Companies, or Watches, had been set up as early as 1667 in an attempt to stamp out the cattle raiding that was widespread in the Highlands. Most of the clans and families who supplied men for the Watches had supported the Hanoverian government against the Jacobites, and the Watches had been made exempt from the ban on Highland garb. The famous regiment, the Black Watch, had its origins in these militia, the name deriving from the dark colour of the tartan, which was so markedly different from 'red coats' of other regiments at the time. (The word 'blackmail' also has its origins in the Highlands, referring to the money paid by cattle owners to clans like the MacGregors in an effort to avoid their livestock being stolen. Black is often used to mean hidden or secret, and may also have referred to the colour of many of the cattle. Mail is an old Scots word for rent or payment.)

A warrior of the MacKenzie clan, by R.R. McIan

The Highland regiments

As the struggle between Britain and France for control of North America flared up into war in 1757, the Prime Minister, William Pitt, decided to commission new Highland regiments to take part. This idea had previously been pursued in 1692, at the time of the Glen Coe massacre, when Gray John, Earl of Breadalbane, had proposed that Highland soldiers fight overseas for the British crown. There had always been a strong tradition of Scottish soldiers serving as mercenaries or military advisors, and the annals of European monarchs and armies are peppered with accounts of Scottish heroism and skill.

Pitt's decision, however, involved a cynicism that causes revulsion even today, since he was motivated by an indifference as to whether or not the Highlanders were killed. The measure also struck at the traditional alliance that had existed between Scotland and France for centuries, particularly before 1707, the year of the Union of the Scottish and English Parliaments. For a period in earlier centuries, Scots and French had held dual citizenship, and Scots had provided the personal bodyguard for the kings of France. This cooperation had persisted in the eighteenth century, and the French had supported the Stuart claims to the British throne during the Jacobite Risings. The defeated Bonnie Prince Charlie escaped to France after the battle of Culloden, and Scots who held commissions in the French army and who had fought for the Jacobites were treated by the British government as formal prisoners of war when captured and not killed out of hand. Even in the Napoleonic Wars there are recorded incidents where as a result of the past links between the two nations, both Scots and French treated one another's prisoners and wounded with chivalrous respect.

The legendary fighting prowess of the Highland regiments, their continued will to wear the kilt and tartan and the standardisation of many tartans in a regimental form all helped to create a mood of general public approval for the removal of the ban on tartan. Another factor, helping to bring about a repeal of the ban, was the character of the new king, George III, who, 20 years after the Rising of 1745, seemed, to those north of the border, less of a foreigner than either George I or George II.

On 17 June 1782, the Marquis of Graham, who helped form the Highland Society of London, appealed to Parliament to move 'that the clause of the nineteenth year of George II, which prohibits the wearing of the Scottish Highland dress, be repealed'. There was only a single dissenting voice, which is still a cause for mirth even today. Sir Philip Jennings Clerke wanted Highland dress to be confined to Scotland because of a story he had been

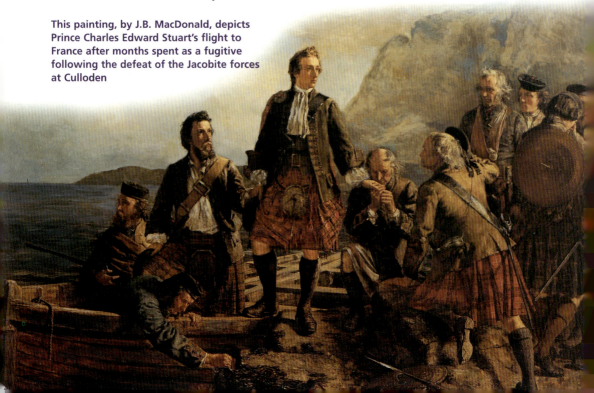

This painting, by J.B. MacDonald, depicts Prince Charles Edward Stuart's flight to France after months spent as a fugitive following the defeat of the Jacobite forces at Culloden

told by a Hampshire innkeeper. When the latter had four Highland officers quartered with him, his wife and daughters had been so taken with the tartans and bare legs of the soldiers that the keeper had to spend the whole time keeping an eye on them.

Rebirth of tartan and associated customs

The end of the ban on tartan was met with wide rejoicing. A Highland proclamation announced:

Listen men! This is bringing before all the Sons of the Gael, that the King and Parliament of Britain have for ever abolished the Act against Highland Dress; which came down to the clans from the beginning of the world to the year 1746. You are no longer bound down to the unmanly dress of the Lowlander. This is declaring to every man, young and old, single and gentle, that they may after this put on and wear the truis, the little kilt, the coat and the striped hose, as also the belted plaid without fear of the law of the realm or the spite of enemies.

The celebrations at the time included such odd spectacles as the Reverend Joseph Robertson Macgregor, the eccentric minister of the Gaelic church in Edinburgh, parading throughout the city clad in a complete suit of tartan. Even today the sideways kicking step of Highland dancers performing the Shean Truis dance is said to symbolise the kicking off of the trews or trousers in favour of the kilt.

However, tartan never recovered as the everyday dress of the Highland population. Perhaps, in some part due to the widespread poverty that the reprisals had brought, many could not afford to buy the new 'manufactured' cloth. The old homespun cottage weaving industry was almost lost forever. A travelling salesman in the Highlands at this time sent a letter to William Wilson of Bannockburn, the first of the new weaving manufacturers, saying that trade was dull, and that he should, '…fill the looms with Officers plaids. There is neither trade nor money here at present!'.

And so it fell to the military to continue the tartan tradition. It was around this time, in the latter part of the eighteenth century, that the famous Highland regiments received their tartans. These included the Cameron Highlanders (Cameron of Erracht tartan), the Seaforth Highlanders (MacKenzie tartan), and the Gordon Highlanders (Gordon tartan). Each of these tartans is a variation of the original Black Watch which dates back to *c.*1739.

Red and white stripes were added to create the Mackenzie tartan

Red stripes (similar to the MacDonald tartan) and yellow were added to create the Cameron of Erracht tartan

A yellow stripe was added to create the Gordon tartan

THE CLAN TARTAN MYTH

Is there really such a thing as a clan tartan, which, in the past, was readily identifiable and which was worn only by its members? If so, are the contemporary clan tartans the same as those worn in the period prior to 1746 and the ban?

These questions were raised, first of all, in the early nineteenth century. Napoleon had been defeated, and the Highland regiments had come home in glory. The issues, then, were as complex as they are today and ranged between two extreme views: that the modern tartans are pure invention or that the patterns worn today are precisely the same as in the heyday of the clans. The truth, however, lies between the two schools of thought. It is certainly a myth that long ago the people of one glen wore a tartan of blue and green, while their neighbours in the next wore red and yellow. Yet, it is the case that the weaving patterns for tartan, the setts, the thread counts and the designs created in one particular area were traditionally associated with it, and a man's clan allegiance could often be identified on the basis of his dress. Martin Martin, a native of Skye and the factor to the MacLeods, wrote a book in 1703 called *Description of the Western Islands of Scotland* in which he said:

A DESCRIPTION OF THE PLAID

The plad wore only by the Men is made of fine Wool, the thread as fine as can be made of that kind: it consists of divers Colours, and there is a great deal of ingenuity requir'd in sorting the Colours, so as to be agreeable to the nicest Fancy. Every Isle differs from each other in their fancy of making plaids, as to the Stripes in Breadth and Colours. This Humour is as different thro' the main Land of the highlands insofar that they who have seen those Places is able at the first view of a Man's Plaid to guess the place of his Residence.

It has also been recorded that in 1703 the laird of Grant ordered that a gathering of 600 of his men should all have tartan coats of the same colour and fashion – red and green.

Further evidence to support the theory that there were some individual 'clan tartans' before 1746 is found in the account of the Battle of Killiecrankie, which took place during the first Jacobite rebellion in 1689, by the bardic chronicler to Viscount Dundee ('Bonnie Dundee'). Here he wrote of Glengarry's men parading in tartan woven in triple stripes, while the men of his brother had a tartan with a red stripe. Maclean of Duart and his brother wore plaids with yellow stripes, and that of McNeil was as bright as a rainbow.

It is also interesting to note that when the Highland regiments were formed in the eighteenth and nineteenth centuries many had new tartans specifically designed for them, some of which were based on older weaving patterns. For example, when Sir Alan Cameron of Erracht (1750–1828) founded the 79th Regiment, the Cameron Highlanders, he designed a new tartan for it and wrote at the time that the main tartan worn in Lochaber before the ban was red in colour. It might be presumed from this that many of the wearers could be identified as Lochaber men and, therefore, probably Camerons.

Evidence of the existence of the Clan Cameron tartan before the '45 comes in the form of the remarkable posthumous painting of the 19th chief. The 'gentle' Locheil was painted by George Chalmers in 1764, 16 years after the chief had died in exile as a result of the wounds at the battle of Culloden. In the context of the times, this portrait made a strong political statement. The exiled chief, swathed in tartan, was not the kind of image that the government of the day sought to encourage. The painting can be seen as an attempt to preserve the culture against proscription and restore the dignity of the defeated rebels.

TARTAN AND THE JACOBITES

Bonnie Prince Charlie was renowned for wearing tartan. He would don the tartan provided by his host at each of the many places he lodged during the '45 campaign, a move by which he intended to encourage the association of the Highland Clans with the Jacobite cause. The Scottish historian, John Telfer Dunbar, recorded over 40 pieces of tartan, held in museums and collections, which are said to have been worn by Bonnie Prince Charlie. Eight of these were supposedly worn at Culloden. What is clear, is that certain tartan patterns were strongly associated with particular clans, families or households, but without specific names. In fact, there are no historic references to clan names for tartans at this time.

A famous painting by David Morier, showing Barrell's regiment facing Highlanders at Culloden, was reputedly painted using Jacobite prisoners as models. Since Morier was George II's military painter and since the work was intended for the Duke of Cumberland, the king's son and brutal military commander, it is widely quoted as evidence for modern clan tartans being bogus. Eight Highlanders in the painting are wearing 23 different tartans. But it could be argued that Morier was simply inaccurate, and that he was not present himself at the battle. Inevitably this debate continues; but it must be said that although there are historical illustrations and paintings showing people in Highland dress, in the belted plaid, the little kilt, truis, or in both, and wearing tartan in profusion, examples of specific clan tartans, named as we know them today, do not exist.

A representation of Prince Charles Edward Stuart wearing the Stuart tartan, by R.R. MacIan

Pettie's painting of Prince Charles Edward Stuart flanked by Lochiel, Chief of Clan Cameron, and Pitsligo, Chief of Clan Forbes.

TOWARDS THE MODERN ERA

Names for Tartans

Recent historic research provides an illustration of how the tartans were named as a result of the Industrial Revolution. William Wilson of Bannockburn was the first of Scotland's weavers to be called a manufacturer. He made the astute discovery that he could increase business by persuading his customers to choose their fabrics

Many different types of tartan are displayed above

from a range of samples, rather than by ordering small quantities of widely differing patterns. In 1777, a receipt appears in Wilson's notebook (which can be seen at the Museum of Scotland in Edinburgh) for 150 ells of tartan cloth, for John and David Gunn, merchants of Forres, 'in your own sett'. (One Scots ell equals 95 centimetres/37 inches.) In the same notebook, but two years later in 1779, orders for 'Gunn' tartan appear for the first time, one for Messrs Hayes of Forres and one for a customer by the name of Squair in Nairn (the next town along the northeast coast from Forres). It seems that the Gunn's of Forres supplied the original pattern, and in subsequent years, others from this locality chose the same pattern from samples carried by Wilson's chapman (salesman). Thus the Gunn tartan was born, with as good a provenance as can be got, for it is possible that the pattern existed, unnamed, for many years prior to the 1777 entry in Wilson's order book.

Fashion Boom

By the nineteenth century, a fashion boom had occurred in tartan, and it became popular attire at high-society balls, both in Britain and abroad. Military tailoring also had a strong effect on Highland dress; garments were given tighter, neater pleats, with coloured stripes falling exactly on the fold of the pleat. Immense public interest was aroused regarding the precise design of family and clan tartans. Colonel David Stewart of Garth produced a classic work called *Sketches of the Character, Manners and Present State of the Highlanders of Scotland, with Details of the Military Service of the Highland Regiments*. He urged a painter of miniatures, Andrew Robertson, to persuade the Highland Society of London to ask chiefs and heads of families to lodge what they considered to be an authentic sample of their own tartan with the society. This presented some difficulty, as many of the Chiefs had no idea of what, exactly, their tartan was supposed to be. Lord MacDonald wrote, on Oct 1 1815, to his clerk, 'Being really ignorant of what is exactly The Macdonald Tartan, I request you will have the goodness to exert every Means in your power to Obtain a perfectly genuine Pattern, Such as Will

Warrant me in Authenticating it with my Arms. Perhaps Sir John Murray May be able to put you in The Way of gaining Some information.'

Logan

James Logan, the son of an Aberdeen merchant, made a study of tartans which produced a level of standardisation. A student of law and art and for a time the secretary of the London Highland Society, he walked around Scotland in 1826 gathering tartan specimens and talking to people who claimed to have authentic first-hand accounts of past practices. He published a valuable work on the subject in 1831, although some of his conclusions have been disputed.

Vestiarium Scoticum

Fact and myth collided in the mid-nineteenth century when the two colourful brothers, John and Charles Sobieski Stuart, who were said to be the legitimate grandsons of Bonnie Prince Charlie appeared in aristocratic society. They claimed to have a sixteenth-century manuscript on which they based a book entitled *Vestiarium Scoticum*, published in 1842. This purported to give the original tartans of the clans. They also produced *The Costume of the Clans* in 1845. The brothers' work, even today, is a cause of much controversy. Their manuscript, said to have been found in the old Scots college at Douai in France, was never produced, and the value of their contribution to tartans research is doubtful. Between 1842 and 1845 another major and popular book appeared. *The Clans of the Scottish Highlands* was largely written by James Logan and illustrated in a highly stylised and romantic form by R.R. McIan.

Above Right: *The Costume of the Clans* by the Sobieski Stuart brothers who claimed to be the grandsons of Prince Charles Edward Stewart

Right: A page from *Vestiarium Scoticum*, which the Sobieski Stuart brothers claimed was based on a sixteenth-century manuscript

This shop window display shows the popularity of tartan

The tartan-producing firms of the nineteenth century started to bring out books of specimens, which ultimately gave rise to the standardisation of family and clan tartans as we know them today. The Lyon Court, Scotland's court for armorial matters, founded in the fourteenth century, also encourages the registration of tartans in its court books. The number of tartans recorded here is very limited and relates solely to the use of tartan as a background to the heraldic 'clan badge'.

One example which has intrigued contemporary researchers came from the pattern books of the Clackmannanshire firm of Patons. An entry from the nineteenth century shows a scrap of largely blue and red tartan with the thread count falling in sevens, entitled 'The 7th Cavalry Tartan'. No British military formation has such a name, although there was an American 7th Cavalry, which achieved fame under General Custer at the Battle of the Little Big Horn, when it was massacred by the Sioux Indians. Apparently, General Custer had a liking for military bands and formed ad hoc brass and bagpipe bands. It is probable that the 7th Cavalry commissioned a tartan for their pipers and drummers, since the regiment contained many Americans of Scottish descent.

Sir Walter Scott by Sir Henry Raeburn

The origins of some tartans may have been questioned, but the overall popularity of the cloth was beyond dispute. Tartan was used for plaids, shawls, blankets, table covers and other commercial items. Even boxes, tins and dishes, known as Mauchline ware, were produced with tartan designs and sent overseas.

Sir Walter Scott

Tartan achieved wider popularity in the nineteenth century through the writings of Sir Walter Scott, who masterminded the famous visit to Edinburgh by George IV in 1822. This was the first monarch to visit Scotland since the Jacobite Rising, and the event was an occasion for great celebration. Heads of families were swathed in tartan, much of it woven in great haste, while the portly Lord Mayor of London, William Curtis, bedecked himself in tartan costume and as the festivities progressed, danced down Princes Street. However, the event placed tartan firmly in the mainstream of Scottish culture, and it is from this time that the kilt evolved into the national costume. Queen Victoria's love of the Highlands also gave the popularity of tartan a boost, and to this day members of the Royal Family wear the kilt when visiting the Highlands.

TARTAN TODAY

A pride in and affection for the tartan is demonstrated by these Scottish football fans, known as the Tartan Army

Tartan's heritage is both glorious and controversial, but what of its current standing and its future? There is a living military tradition, which has ensured that Highland dress and tartan are respected and often revered. There was uproar, for example, amongst the Scottish regiments when the War Office decreed in the Second World War that the kilt was not a suitable campaigning garment. Some soldiers organised protest bonfires and others insisted on taking the kilt with them into action in spite of the ruling. Individuals have worn the kilt into battle in many modern wars, but the last kilted unit, operating as an organised body, was a platoon of the Cameron Highlanders, which fought a heroic rearguard action at Dunkirk in 1940. This occasion, however, ended a tradition of over 1,000 years.

There is continued affection for tartan among Scottish football and rugby supporters, who often flaunt it with immense enthusiasm. There are also growing numbers of pipe bands and Highland dancers, while the kilt is a favourite garment for weddings. It has always been popular dress at musical festivals and ceilidhs, and one senses an increase in the wearing of the kilt for other social occasions, particularly among young people.

Young Highland dancers at the Stonehaven Games

The kilt and its accoutrements

The kilt is a comfortable garment, warm in winter and cool in summer, and a good example should last for generations. There is no pattern for making a kilt. It is a craft learned by apprentices over many months, before they can be awarded the title of 'kiltmaker'.

The modern man in Highland dress may also wear a Balmoral hat, which is rather like a beret and is generally blue – a link to the famous 'blue bonnets' that were part of the campaigning dress of many Scots, and particularly of Highlanders. Sometimes Balmorals have a diced pattern round the rim. This is a relic of an old accounting system that was taken into the heraldry of the Stewarts or High Stewards of Scotland and became known as the 'checky', from which the word 'exchequer' derives. Scottish policemen also wear this pattern, a symbol of guardianship and protection. The boat-shaped Glengarry hats are of nineteenth-century military origin.

Shirts, jackets and ties are entirely a matter of taste, although tweed jackets (largely green or brown) for daytime wear and black for evening wear, with rather more ornate shirts and accessories, are generally the custom.

In the past, belts were normally made of leather with brass buckles, but now there is a whole variety of designs and materials. Sporrans (the Gaelic word for purse) were once worn on the hip and had strings instead of studs. Sporrans are produced using synthetic materials following old designs, which were formerly executed in seal, goat or

Below left: A kiltmaker at work

Below: This dancer's kilt is weighted down with the kilt pin, which resulted mainly from Queen Victoria's desire to preserve the modesty of her soldiers

deer skin. The kilt pin dates from the nineteenth century, and largely resulted from the desire of Queen Victoria and her senior military staff to preserve the modesty of her soldiers. The pin is used only as a weight and is not pinned through to the inner apron. Underwear beneath the kilt – so often a cause for humour – is a relatively modern development, and in the past men wore nothing. This is still true of several Scottish regiments, apart from some sentries and dancers, on whom the kilt might fly up. Most other people wear shorts or pants, according to personal taste.

Below: The sgian dubh was once used as an implement for skinning and eating, but is now mainly decorative. Similarly the flashes at the sides of the sock are symbolic of the ribbon garter worn in times past. The panel (right) shows tartan accessories available by the early twentieth century

Of the other Highland dress accessories, knitted socks are also a relatively recent innovation. In the past, hose were made from the same material as the kilt. The small flashes at each side of the stockings are symbolic of the kind of ribbon-garter that was used in the past and tied with a special knot. Shoes, like socks, are a matter of personal preference. The convention for evening wear, however, is black with the laces tied around the ankle. The Gaelic for shoe is *brog* from which comes the English word brogue. The holes that are often punched in the leather symbolise the holes made in deer-hide footwear to let water out. (The Gaelic words for 'my footwear' are *mo chasan*, and it has been suggested that Scottish migrants to North America who used this word might have given rise to the Indian word moccasin.) The small knife tucked into the stocking is called a *sgian dubh*, or black knife, and was originally an implement for eating or skinning, although nowadays it is mainly decorative. The adjective 'black' derives from the use of coarse metal, rather than the prized shining metal used for weapons. Some people wear ornamental dirks attached to their belts for evening wear.

It is undoubtedly the case that a Highlander from many centuries ago should he see the dress of his nineteenth-, twentieth- and twenty-first century descendants, would recognise his own garb.

A form of Highland dress in the modern era

Tartan styles for women

Early Highland women wore a longer version of the man's shirt and then had a version of the man's belted plaid, known as the arisaid. It was made of tartan and white was generally the predominant colour. The garment reached down to the ground and was fixed at the waist with a belt and fastened with a pin at the breast. There was sufficient loose cloth to pull over the head like a hood in bad weather and underneath a full petticoat was worn. Occasionally an additional shawl was used. Modern conventions on the use of tartan sashes and plaid-type sashes, or brooches, are largely a matter of taste, but you may wish to refer to instructions of a former Lord Lyon, Sir Thomas Innes of Learney.

Above: Traditional tartan patterns have influenced modern dress and even *haute couture*

Left: A woman of the MacNicol clan in a traditional form of Highland dress for women

The correct way to wear ladies sashes

These three versions have the approval of Sir Thomas Innes of Learney, one time Lord Lyon King of Arms. They also appear in Frank Adams' book, *The Clans Septs and Regiments of the Scottish Highlands*, and in *Tartans and Highland Dress* by MacKinnon of Dunakin.

The sash is worn over the right shoulder, across the breast and secured by a brooch on the right shoulder. This style is worn by clanswomen, women of the clan surname and septs by birth or marriage.

The sash is worn over the left shoulder, across the right breast and secured with a brooch on the left shoulder. This style is worn by Lady Chiefs, chieftainesses, the wives of clan chiefs and chieftains, and the wives of colonels of Highland regiments.

The sash is worn over the right shoulder and tied in a bow, or secured with a pin, at the waist on the left. This style is worn by ladies who have married out of their clan but who still wish to use their original clan tartan.

New tartans

There are now many new tartans, some of which are extremely attractive. For example, there are tartans for some American states and Canadian provinces, for overseas military units and bands, for special anniversaries, for civilian organisations such as the City of Glasgow, even for fire brigades and airlines.

Tartan enthusiasts owe a great debt to modern scholars who pioneered the system of filing tartan samples and pedigrees, who researched district tartans, and who gradually separated myth from fact. Tartan is a living subject, and the regard for this part of Scotland's heritage and the beauty of the subject matter are not in doubt.

There is a heartwarming zest of Scots overseas for the kilt and tartan that has a strong beneficial effect on those who wear the kilt in Scotland. In America, for example, there is a charming custom called 'the kirking of the tartan', which means to have the cloth blessed in church. The American astronaut Alan L. Bean even took a piece of MacBean tartan to the moon and back, which shows the depth of feeling for this special and internationally known cloth.

The Scottish writer Neil Munro wrote a poem called 'The Kilt is my Delight', which became the title of a television programme. The kilt can be your delight as well.

Pipers wearing kilts are a familiar and popular sight with visitors to Scotland

LITTLE KNOWN FACTS ABOUT TARTANS

Finzean's Fancy
Archibald Farquharson of Finzean (pronounced fingin) designed this sett to promote his claim to the chiefship of Clan Farquharson c.1805–15 and his bid to become a Member of Parliament. He based his design on the Chattan Chief's sett, making clear his political alignment and possibly his aspirations. A complete tartan outfit including a tartan jacket can be seen at the Stonehaven Museum, one of several in which Finzean clothed his personal bodyguard.

Flower of Scotland
Designed as a tribute to Roy Williamson, writer of the words and music of 'The Flower of Scotland', Scotland's alternative national anthem. Roy wore the Gunn tartan, which has been used as the framework of the new tartan. Cornflower blue and Zephyr green have been used to suggest the bluebell and the thistle. (UK Registered Design No.600421.)

Forsyth tartan
This sett has a close resemblance to the Leslie tartan in which white replaces yellow. A description of the tartan appears in Jennie Forsyth Jeffrie's *History of the Forsyth Family* (1918). Clan Chief, Alistair Forsyth, was recognised by Lord Lyon in 1978 – the first for over 300 years.

Fraser Hunting
In the Hunting Fraser, brown replaces the red of the Clan sett. The late Charles Ian Fraser of Reeling said, in his publication, 'Clan Fraser', that this sett was designed by the Sobieski Stuart brothers at the request of Lord Lovat for use by the Inverness and Nairn militia. A letter to Lord Lovat from the War Office, c.1855, authorised the use of the Fraser tartan for the corps.

Hannay tartan
The Hannay tartan has been long established in the South West of Scotland. An old kilt worn by Commander Alex Hannay (1788–1844) was discovered by his descendant, Miss Anne Hannay, in the family chest and came into the possession of Councillor John Hannay, a well-known tartan designer and collector. He created a new design based on the old, which included a red stripe. Messrs Galt of Galloway produced this sett around 1950. The black and white check is a common feature of Lowland tartans, originally woven with the undyed wool and found in the earliest of tartans, the 'Shepherds Plaid'. It is interesting to note that the colours of the armorial bearings of the Chiefly House of Hannay of Scorbie are Sable, Argent and Azure – black, silver and blue.

Hepburn tartan
Anderson's of Edinburgh produced this sett for Captain Charles Hepburn in 1968, from an existing design. Hepburns are associated with Hermitage Castle in Liddesdale and the history of Mary Queen of Scots. James Hepburn, 4th Earl of Bothwell (1536–78), married the Queen after being implicated in the murder of her husband, Henry Stewart, Lord Darnley.

The Hannay clan have had associations with the southwest of Scotland since the thirteenth century, and the black and white check is a feature of the Lowland tartans

The Shepherd's Plaid is one of the earliest of tartans, woven with undyed wool

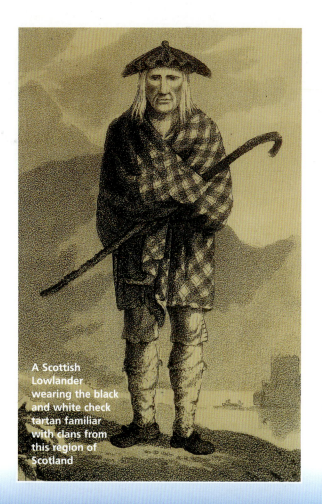

A Scottish Lowlander wearing the black and white check tartan familiar with clans from this region of Scotland

Holyrood tartan

Holyrood is the Scottish equivalent of Buckingham Palace, the monarch's official residence in Scotland. She is guarded by 'The Royal Company of Archers', a non-military force provided by the chiefs of the clans and prominent citizens. Lochcarron Weavers presented a sample of the Holyrood tartan to the Scottish Tartans Society in 1980.

Morrison tartan

Lord Lyon recorded the official Morrison clan tartan on 3 January 1968, from a piece of tartan cloth found in an old Morrison family bible. The bible contained a hand written reference to the tartan and was dated 1747, one year after the proscription of Highland dress. The discovery was made during the demolition of a Black House on Lewis in 1935. Lord Lyon was convinced that it represented the most authentic pattern of what the Morrisons wore in those days and he based the new tartan on the relic.

Below: Holyrood Palace in Edinburgh, the monarch's official residence in Scotland. The Holyrood tartan was presented to the Scottish Tartans Society in 1980